Blessing for the Unborn

poems by

Anna Lowe Weber

Finishing Line Press
Georgetown, Kentucky

Blessing for the Unborn

For Lila and Charlie

Copyright © 2017 by Anna Lowe Weber
ISBN 978-1-63534-114-0 First Edition
All rights reserved under International and Pan-American Copyright Conventions.
No part of this book may be reproduced in any manner whatsoever without written permission from the publisher, except in the case of brief quotations embodied in critical articles and reviews.

ACKNOWLEDGMENTS

Instinct, Fresh Envy: *Hoot and Hare Review*
Blessing for the Unborn: *Salamander*
When You Ask to Hear the Story of Your Birth: *Reunion: The Dallas Review*
On My First Valentine's Day after Giving Birth: A Sonnet for My Husband: *The Sonnets, Hermeneutic Chaos Press*
At the Little Gym: *The Mom Egg*
Bombs in Springtime: *Ascent*
Toddler: *The Beechwood Review*
The Blood: *The McNeese Review*
How Do I Braid it into My Very Being, Child?: *The Boiler Journal*
Before You Had a Name: *Kentucky Review*
Dwell: *Makeout Creek*

Publisher: Leah Maines

Editor: Christen Kincaid

Cover Art: Kathryn Jill Johnson

Author Photo: Ryan Weber

Cover Design: Elizabeth Maines

Printed in the USA on acid-free paper.
Order online: www.finishinglinepress.com
　　　　　also available on amazon.com

Author inquiries and mail orders:
Finishing Line Press
P. O. Box 1626
Georgetown, Kentucky 40324
U. S. A.

Table of Contents

The Conception 1
Instinct 2
Host 3
Quickening 4
Blessing for the Unborn 5
When you ask to hear the story of your birth 6
On My First Valentine's Day after Giving Birth:
    A Sonnet for My Husband 8
Daughter 9
At the Little Gym 10
Alabama Winter 12
Bombs in Springtime 13
After Boston 15
Fresh Envy 17
Our Fourth Anniversary, On Which I Have Forgotten
    to Get You a Card or a Present 19
Childproof 20
Toddler 22
Girls 23
At Three You Are 25
How Do I Braid It Into My Very Being, Child? 26
Trying to Conceive 27
The Blood 29
No Luck with Western Medicine 30
In the room 31
The Second Time Around 32
Before You Had a Name 33
Dwell 34

The Conception

Because our breath bent
as wind bends. Because sugar
not salt. Because one of us
asked nicely.

Because love came
in the form of a tiny ship
which we pulled back and forth
through the bathwater.
Because we clapped our hands and said
Merrily. Merrily. Merrily. Merrily.

Because of me not you. Or
you not me. Or the dog who
now begs at the door morning
after morning.

Because of the rosemary and thyme,
holding the backyard hostage, or
Saint Gabriel, plunged into the ground
headfirst alongside the monkey grass.

Monkey grass, we call on you.
Saint of Conception, we call on you.
Herbs and bathwater and dog, heed
our prayers. It whines and it whines—
all that we keep out and let in.

Instinct

I knew.
Even when I didn't know, I knew.
Compelled to sleep
in the middle of the day
on the hardwood floors
of our new home, I knew
some yellow-bellied sprout
was taking root. I woke
to a white web spreading, needling
my insides. How to not feel
that weather shift?
Molecules rearranging themselves
into a tempest. Trees shuddering
their leaves at once to reveal hundreds
of birds. Or just one.
Swelled in song.

Host

Here you have created within me
a place for yourself, meat and mucous
and skin. Slice of pickled cartilage.
Palest follicle. Tiny seahorse suspended
in a tiny jar. *Hippocampus Erectus*. Here
is your fiddlehead fern of a tail. Spiny
dragon's head. You are crushable,
tender bone and rings, scales stretched
over a pink nothing. You are all storm
and no wrath, soothed to sleep again
and again by waves that never break.

Quickening

What the words *vanishing point* and *distance*
mean will change—I know this—
in the moment I first hold you to my chest,
unearthed from my body in gut. In blood.
I watch my belly ripen every hour. I want
to identify the ripples: hand. Foot. And call you
sweet thing now, while you are still mine.
Your voice my own, a caverned body echo.
My veins work overtime, thick blue maplines
marking boundaries and edges I'll spend my life
trying to cross.

This is what I want to keep from you,
just for a little while: the lines
the ugly world is full of, red hems and horizons
and ruler ticks by which you'll be made
to measure your days. I'd like to hide
how quickly you might flounder, thrash
in shallow water. How easily any of us fail,
and daily. Swim deep now. Each broad stroke
a blow to my insides. A painful reminder of
what little time I have left to contain you
in only myself.

Blessing for the Unborn

I want to tell you now: you are not between worlds.
You are no marble figure. Swallows take no flight
from your mouth. Nothing bursts forth.
And while I have you, let me say: you will not rise
from the salt mounds. Your hair will stay
the color of dishwater, will reek of dinge and
yellowed particle. All flake. Sweet child,
while I have you, we can say together: Hello,
grimy world. Hello suture and blotch. Child,
these are the stains I have handed to you.
These are the imperfections. Here is the
chipped pearl among the strand. And while I
have you, may you roll it in your hands.
Own it. Warm it in the heat from your palms.

When you ask to hear the story of your birth

I will tell you: you were late. The ultrasound image
on your due date revealed you to be a cramped thing—

your face, a flattened blur in shades of black and gray,
squashed against my confines. Your body, crowding mine.

Oh, she's plenty comfy in there, the nurse crowed, wiping away
the gel from my belly globe. And so we went home and waited

for another week. Child, you were late. How many times
did we summon you? How many times did I call out?

Come out, come out. How adept you were already at ignoring
my voice, snubbing my pleas. Stubborn, willful thing.

When you ask to hear the story of your birth,
I will lie. I will not tell you how I loathed those last few days.

I will tell you that I told you to take your time.
That I respected the hours that you needed. That each night

as I spoke your name, I anointed my body with oils,
heating them first in my hands before greasing up

that stretched, shiny middle of mine. I will lie and tell you
I was gentle with your soul, but child: I was not.

How badly I wanted to be done with the whole thing.
I drank wine in the bathtub. I pictured you making your way

through the red walls and corridors of my body.
These, the last hours I ever kept you in my clutches.

And I will tell you something true: I cried when they pressed you to my chest. For when you finally crawled out—so slick, so awake—

those bird-dark eyes taking in every bit of the world they landed on—
your journey away from me had already begun.

On My First Valentine's Day after Giving Birth: A Sonnet for My Husband

This is my request: please take me even though my stomach
puddles. Please take me with my flabby jowls of thigh.
Love, I know my hair has gone to shit. Take it. And my
ankles, for yes, even they've gained weight. They ache.
My feet—nights, they swell like bloated boats. Can you make
them your own, even so? I wish you'd at least give it a try.
Kiss this body, this overgrown landscape, the yellow-dry
grass, the shrubs gone wild and green. For the sun must break
over it each morning just the same—it spreads wide and gold
across the ugliest plots of land. Leaves no garden cold,
however foul the flowers. So please love, take your plow
and till, rake, hoe. Cultivate my hips gone wide with birth.
My breasts, they sag and wilt, but love, might you still sow
your seed? Fling, plant, spread. This body yours to unearth.

Daughter

 In your lifespan, many fools will speak

of equations. Know this: even before your arrival,

my arms were always open, an equal sign hinging

from my body. Lifted to some spirit of arithmetic

I couldn't name. Casting light on angles and shapes,

the disappearing zeroes of green valleys.

 Now I know the reckoning of blood

and new life, thick between my legs. The way

slick hair cries: dark and sweetly as an overripe stone fruit.

I know the mathematics between a first breath

and a last.

 Daughter, calculate the number of drops

of rain the average human mouth can hold, then

sit with me on the back porch. We can tilt

our faces to the gray dim as the clouds roll onto

their stomachs. To the approaching storm,

smaller frogs will offer one voice, a swollen veil

of yellow croaks.

At the Little Gym

The absurdity of it doesn't escape me:
        a gymnastics class for babies. When
you are very young, we simply sit together

on the giant blue mat. I prop you up
        against my legs like a sack of potatoes,
and at the instructor's command, I stretch

your legs and arms: in and out. Back
        and forth. Up and down. In and out.
Some trippy version of the alphabet song

blares from the stereo, and intermittently,
        a man's voice offers advice: *Stretching
is vital for gross motor skill development...*

*Remember moms and dads: it's impossible
        to love your baby too much...* I'm not sure if
I agree with that, but before I can reflect on it,

the class moves on and suddenly
        all of the babies are being lifted up,
hoisted onto our shoulders, paraded

across the room like show-dogs.
        It's too much for one of them, and she
begins to whimper—softly at first.

A quiet complaint. But then it swells
        into a cry, a wail, a tornado siren filling
the room with its red blare. We exchange

looks of pity with each other as the mother
        hauls the baby out. Hey, we've all been there.
Today, I am grateful for your silence.

The man on the stereo is saying something
        about the magic of the inner ear. I place
you back on the blue mat alongside

the other babies. Watch as you all seem
        to drift towards some indecipherable point,
fish endlessly floating with an invisible current.

Alabama Winter

Which is to say: not really winter. Some humid
        gray intermediate. Air still warm enough to breathe
without pain. Never cold enough to pilfer. Never

that cold that seeps to your core, fractures bones
        into splinters that refuse to heal. It was winter in the South,
so: none of that. Still we built fires. Still the smoke crawled

out of our chimney, lingered in the moist air
        like a lazy animal, some cow always lounging in the fields
behind our house. Moo, we said to the cow, passing him

on our way to the store. Sometimes, even in winter, it was
        warm enough to crank the windows down. Everything
around us seemed muted, a photograph stripped of color.

Insipid imitations of greens and reds and blues. Still
        we mooed. What does a cow say? What color is the grass?
Even as a child, you knew that the sun wasn't quite yellow.

January days it burned a hole in the sky. The light it gave
        was practically nothing, but there we were—turning
our faces towards it again and again.

Bombs in Springtime

We were lost in the yellow of spring
        when the bombs went off. All over
our backyard, irises were erupting

from the ground, laying claim onto
        whatever sliver of life their only week
on earth could offer before the season

moved on. When the bombs went off,
        we moved boxes from one house to another.
We spent the week sorting, packing, taping,

lifting. We were moving. We were trading
        one life for another when the bombs went
off. New house, new neighborhood.

We were fielding invitations to attend
        the local Baptist church. We were trying
to change the subject. We were watching tv

reports. Shaking our heads. When the bombs
        went off, the news always found us.
Our child hung around, restless. She

shuffled her feet. When the bombs went off,
        she was outside shaking pink blossoms down
from the redbud tree. At least

we thought it was a redbud. We were accepting
        pan after pan of neighborly
lasagna. Not telling anyone that we didn't

eat meat. We were lying by omission. When
        the bombs went off, we were pretending to sleep
on a mattress in the middle of our new

bedroom. It was the yellow of spring.
          Irises were erupting. Anther and
filament knew nothing but to quiver

as voices rose in the streets, some game
          of stick ball breaking out between the kids
who were allowed to stay out past dark.

After Boston

Pushing my daughter in her stroller
       around our new neighborhood's
man-made lake, we stumble upon a fish.

Huge. Dead. Muted glass eye seeing
       nothing. So dead he appears to be fused
with the land, growing out of the mossy banks

of the lake, or emerging from the sandy,
       algae-furried shore like a 1950's cinematic
swamp monster, killed mid-crawl by the hero

of the movie. His scales, oversized paillettes
       with no shine left to give. Even settled in the stroller,
my daughter sees the fish coming—Dah! Dah! Dah is

everything—the window on the far side
       of her bedroom when she wakes, the dog,
constant and ever-patient under her high chair,

her favorite stuffed bunny. Dah is mama. Dah
       is dada. Dah is the dead fish. Dah! No, sweet girl,
I tell her. We can't get out and see

the fish. We need to keep moving,
       keep strolling, keep towards home. And
we do. But days later, I can't stop

thinking about the fish. Thinking
       that maybe we should have stopped after all.
Should have studied his ugly face: the thin

white mouth dry, agape as if the death
       somehow came as a surprise. His body, refusing
to be anything but waterlogged, colorless.

I should have made her stare, I think. Made
        her point—dah. Repulsive. Foul. Look,
little girl. Look at the nasty this world

can come up with, given half the chance.
        The day after our walk, someone blows up bodies
in an American city. And we run in circles

of people who say, Listen, this happens
        every day in other countries. Other countries,
I want to say. I want to say: let me be

ignorant. But I don't. I keep quiet. We watch
        the news reports over and over. She points
at the screen. Dah. Dah. Please, let me walk away.

Fresh Envy

I cannot figure out the difference
        between lime green and new lime
and bright lime and limelight. Sounds

of nature. Tasty apple. Clean scent
        green. Paradise. Yew green—what
does that one mean? Green sheep? You

trail the aisles of Home Depot with our
        shrieking baby while the salesman
talks at me about undertones, palettes,

the mood of the room or the room
        of the mood—I'm not sure. I stopped
listening hours ago. I'm still trying

to figure out the whole yew thing
        when it hits me—I'm thinking of
ewe. And thinking of you, you with

the baby who seems now to prefer
        you over me. Squeals when she
sees you, runs (or tries to) toward you

when you enter a room. You,
        you, you, I try not to think. I try
to hold my head high, to remember

that article from whatever parent magazine
        sat tattered in the pediatrician's
office—Babies go through phases. *They often*

prefer one parent over the other, for no real
        reason at all. Try not to indulge in
spousal envy, the article advised. But how could I

not feel envious, with the way she calls
        for you, reaches out with those baby-fat arms,
grabs your beard in her hands and pulls?

By the time you come back around
        from the chandelier and ceiling fan aisle,
she is laughing again, grabbing

that beard, grabbing handfuls of
        paint sample cards and tossing them
into the air like oversized confetti.

Happy new year, I tell the salesman,
        trying to remember why we decided to paint
the living room green in the first place.

Our Fourth Anniversary, On Which I Have Forgotten to Get You a Card or a Present

So instead I point to our daughter,
now a little over a year old. There, I say.
I got you that. I gave birth to that.
Happy Anniversary. She's running
now, always and everywhere, and
doesn't bother putting on the brakes
to listen to whatever adult syllables
are being strung together by her idiot
parents. That's how I imagine
she thinks of us, already—*my idiot parents.*
One always grousing about something.
One kindly but meek. She's hurtling herself
through the air—bounding across
the backyard like some sort of prairie
beast. And I want to grab her arm,
to give her pause. Hey listen, I want
to say—we weren't always like this.
There were other anniversaries with
bathtubs of champagne. We were
fucking Gatsby, for Christ's sake.
But she'll never believe me. The lie
that your parents never truly lived
before you came long is one that all children
must tell themselves in order to exist.
She's off again, having spotted a jam
of fireflies in one corner of the yard.
It has not yet occurred to her that
there might be something—anything—
in this world that does not belong to her.
This always-hungry child. This universe
expanding still and still and still.

Childproof

Because she figured out that no one
was watching. Took advantage of that
yellow glow of distraction. Because
there has to be a line where distraction
turns to negligence, and certainly we
were dancing it, pouring wine after a long day
and thanking god that for once, the house
seemed blessedly quiet. Because she was
upstairs, reading. And then she wasn't.
She figured out how easily she could stretch
to the tips of her toes to reach the front door's
cheap gold knob. You'll want to have those
replaced, our realtor had told us. Because
we never do anything quickly. Because
the wine was coating our throats so nicely
that neither of us heard the door swing open.
Because it opened to late-summer grass
that still smelled green, and even a toddler
can appreciate the sanctity of freedom.

    She did not make it to the highway,
or the lake down the road, though I can imagine
that she did. I can force my tongue up against
that ulcer: the floating body; the paralyzing pause
before a truck makes contact. We found her
ten feet in front of the house, sitting on the sidewalk.
Watching the cars as they passed and offering
a casual wave. Lifting her shirt to flaunt
her belly button—*get a load of this*. Because
we learned what it means when people say
"It happened so quickly." We learned that
the vilest ugly the world can dole out
is given not in years, or days, or hours even,
but seconds. The relief that washes over you
will be short-lived, because you are doomed
to play the "what if" game for the rest of your life.

Doomed to wonder when whoever
it was that you out-tricked, outran, outplayed
that evening as you sprinted to the curb and clung
to every warm inch of body the child could give—
when they will catch up to claim what was
rightfully theirs for the taking.

Toddler

She is quite taken with him,
this talking television tiger.
Don't you think it's strange,
I ask, that he only wears a hoodie
but no pants? Isn't it strange
that a tiger is best friends
with a housecat and a prince?
She ignores me, which seems right.
Already at only two, she is adept
at tuning me out. At night, bath-soft
and smelling of soap and honey
and pistachio cream, snug as a bug
in her pink princess pajamas,
she strokes my face gently and says,
"Sometimes I don't like you very much."

Girls

The water must be freezing
between their legs, the way
these girls squeal. The way
they scream. We hike alongside
the river they float down,
an endless line of plastic ducks,
bobbing and dipping in cola-colored
water. They have wrapped their
miniscule t-shirts around their heads
like jewel-colored turbans. To keep
the sun off? Who knows why
girls do what they do. You are
just over two, walking alongside me
on the trail instead of perched
in the backpack. My back is happy for it,
but you look so small as you run,
then hang back to pick another flower.
Do you need to go potty? I ask
for the fourth time. You shake your head
no, and I'm glad—unsure what I would do
if the answer were yes. Crouch with you
on the trail? Another girl flies
down the river. Careful, I say—
not too close to the edge. You're
dancing the line and you know it. Do you
want to get back in the backpack?
Half question, half threat.

You shake your head no,
and we continue on the trail. One of the girls
has started singing a song. I don't recognize it,
but you stop, cock your head and listen.
For a minute, I think you, too, are going
to start singing. Erupt into lyrics
that I never knew you knew. Scary
everything you're picking up at this age.

But no. You haven't stopped to sing,
but to uproot yet another flower.
And part of me wants to stop hiking,
to sit and pick flowers
for the rest of the afternoon.
To show you how to make a chain
from white clover. Where to split
the stem exactly so that it opens
but doesn't break. A tear just large enough
to slip the next blossom through.
Don't all girls learn this, eventually?
Didn't we all spend afternoons
sweaty in the sun, growing our chains
longer and longer? Adorning ourselves
with their drape and shackle. Singing
some song our mothers never could
figure out the words to.

At Three You Are

Angry, sometimes it seems
all the time. You are doors
slamming, a body hurled
to the floor, a live web
of sparked wires
firing off all at once.
Where does fury
hide in such a tiny, tender
figure? I see fire coursing
through your small limbs,
the ones you fling
around my neck just as quickly,
eager to secure forgiveness.
All's well that ends, but in
the night, claiming monsters,
your body is a furnace
pressed tight against my own
and I feel your wrath feeding.
It blooms and breeds, multiplies
as rapidly as the cells that grow
your body exponentially,
it seems, overnight. Doubling and
doubling. At three, you are hell
to share a bed with. Still, I can't
turn you away.

How Do I Braid it into My Very Being, Child?

Mornings, your hair in wild ropes.
Your colt-sweet limbs, the way they
wrap and tangle, seek warmth
in my own arms and legs which always seem
too clumsy, too pale by comparison.
My stodgy adult body, and you, brown berry child,
pressed into it. What is the countdown
for how long this will last? Another year?
A week? Time is always ripping you away
from me like the old cliche—a bandaid pulled
so slowly that at first, it might seem insignificant.
But here are the bits of skin and hair that
lift away with the bandage. Here I twinge,
grit my teeth. One morning you stop
asking me, "rub my belly." Your body
is yours, and I know, I know—it always
has been. Whatever ownership I felt
was wrong, even when you housed yourself
in me, your tadpole speck eyes, poppy-seeds
learning to blink. I penned valentines to you—
Be Mine. A wish, or a command.
But you weren't; not really.
Now your voice rises in impatience
some mornings. Demands are made for
breakfast, a show about ponies. You sit
on the couch, a foot taller overnight.
And when I stare, you are three going on
thirty. What? you ask. I sit too.
Your body, burning. Buzzing
with growth even as I shrink away
to nothing. To a withered seed, some day
you'll bury.

Trying to Conceive

After many months, still nothing. I picture
my uterus, an egg without a yolk. Filled with

some slick, spittle fluid of zilch. Wind egg,
it's called. No jewel to be hatched. One day,

I think, the yolk will show up—hearty and
radiant-orange. One day you will crack me

to find life inside, awake and kicking. But
today is not that day. And we are not allowed

to be sad because we have one child already—
perfectly healthy and strong. Exuberant even.

Don't be selfish, we think. To ask for more
than what we already have? That's just greedy.

No one likes a glutton. So we swallow
it down, live in that special misery of wanting

what you can't have and don't even need.
Now that we want another one, I find

that babies are everywhere. Out in public, I stare
and ogle. Even as the mother catches my eye,

turns to shield her baby from my unrelenting gaze—
even then, I can see the back of the head,

downy blonde and supple. The two fontanels
that haven't yet merged, the soft spot

that pumps a slight pulse with the beat
of the infant's heart. How I used to crave that spot

on my own child—a reminder that she still
wasn't quite of this world. A vulnerability

at once delicious and terrifying, lingering
under the gentle stroke of my thumb.

The Blood

It was Maisie or Clara or Cecelia. It was
Rebecca. It was a dull ache in the body's
back-lit pit, a small throb swelling outward
until you knew it was coming,
expelled from you like a magician's red scarf.
It was Natalie or June or Stella. It was a girl,
always, because who else could betray
you like that, month after month? Who
escapes childhood without an understanding
that girls are the cruelest, the most cutting?
Who else would inflict such a wound?
After a while, it was a letter from god:
fuck you. And it was a letter you penned
to your body, whatever gland or ketone
was off, whatever organ wasn't quite
up to snuff. It was the carousel at the mall,
the way the children squealed, clamped
their hands around the thick, glossy necks of
fiberglass lions and tigers, the horses
with their garish smiles revealing an extra set
of teeth. It was Marnie. It was Tess.
It was Grace, the way you imagined her
nestled in the crook of your arm on a Sunday,
or collapsing into you on a summer night,
the yard alight with insects that were biting,
drawing blood, wondering what it was about yours
that tasted so bitterly of iron and pity and grief.

No Luck with Western Medicine

Despite the white pills doled out like candy
by my doctor. So we go East. Mornings now,
twice a week, I recline on the acupuncturist's table,
answer questions about cycles and sleep patterns
and anxiety under the orange glow of the heat lamp.
He talks about chi, body energy. And I swallow hard
because another friend has announced another pregnancy.
I'm preoccupied with my reaction—was I happy enough?
Too happy? Manic? At least I didn't cry until I got to my car.
He inserts the needles in quick succession—ankles, stomach,
ears and scalp. I've become the person no one wants
to share good news with.

He says I will not bleed, but when the treatment is over
and I am left alone to rise from the table, clambering off
the butcher paper with its deafening folds and creases,
I check the mirror. Where my hair is parted, my scalp
is not flesh-colored but crimson, a deep shock of red
lining my pate like a river. Dark-drying stain.
Another blot, this blood—as with the other,
a marker of what won't be mine.

In the room

We wait. They draw blood and
blood and blood for weeks until
the inner-crook of my arm boasts
a knobby blue bead, a tiny pebble
where the blood has leaked
into the surrounding skin. It refuses
to retreat. It will blossom a lovely bruise,
I know. That was a difficult stick,
the nurse says. Make a fist, then release it.
After months, they still can't tell us anything.
No reason why the thread refuses
to slip through the needle's eye.

The Second Time Around

Everything feels less tenuous.
Your sister, our firstborn, I imagined
delicate as filament, a dandelion clock
barely protected from some kid's hot,
eager breath. But second child, mere days
into our life together and already I trust
in your sturdiness. I'll try to paint it
as time-earned knowledge, a comfort
won only through experience. More likely,
it's simple laziness. I forget to read labels,
steal sips of wine and coffee even in these,
the earliest weeks. It's so hard to remember
which cheeses are not allowed. Soon after
it's been recalled, I eat ice cream from a brand
supposedly tainted with listeria. What is it,
this blind faith I have in your life?
This foolish confidence in your survival?

      It is the blight of the second child
to always come up smiling. The burden
you owe creation is one of capability.
I know, already: you will be what people call
an easy baby. But it is not ease as much as it is
an eventual resignation. Your cries will often go
ignored, unheeded until they dwindle into
accepted silence. Second child, my apologies
in advance, for what I already know: your firsts
will go unrecorded. Smiles and steps will vanish,
disappear into the world like the dandelion's
downy seeded tufts, an afternoon's wish
made and forgotten by dusk.

Before you had a name

       Bone-man I called you. I called you blink,
belly shudder, tag-along. Weren't you a minnow

       then, swimming against the stream? I called you
mine but that's a laugh, right? A spinning yarn,

       the story all parents wear like a hairshirt—close
to the skin and constant in its hurt,

       a bleat you can't unhear. Listen to the lie—the way
it goes on, kvetching in the night. Even at your smallest,

       a clump of cells in bloom, proliferation in rapid time
lapse—
even then, the fibs you told were real whoppers.

       I'm yours. I'm yours. Grow me right
and I'll never leave you.

Dwell

Babe asleep in the crib, walnuts
at delicate rest atop her eyelids
until sunrise. You carve our names
into the underbelly of the kitchen table
and I watch from tangled sheets,
bowl of overripe figs in my lap,
trying to extract a bit more sweetness
from that which so long ago went
black. In a house up the road,
someone has my heart in a bedside jar.
Root tuber heart. It is starting to sprout.
To cover itself with crisp yellow vines
and blind eyes and buds.

Anna Lowe Weber, originally from Louisiana, lives with her husband, daughter, and son in Huntsville, Alabama, where she teaches creative writing for the University of Alabama in Huntsville. She has an MFA in poetry from Purdue University, and has had poetry featured or forthcoming in *Rattle, The Florida Review, The Iowa Review, Salamander,* and *Ninth Letter,* among other journals. Her poetry has been nominated for a Pushcart Prize, and her poem "Spring Break 2011" was a finalist for the Rattle Poetry Prize.

www.ingramcontent.com/pod-product-compliance
Lightning Source LLC
LaVergne TN
LVHW041600070426
835507LV00011B/1204